DISCARD

THE BATTLE OF
MONMOUTH

Lewis K. Parker

BLACKBIRCH®
PRESS

THOMSON
━━━━━✶━━━━━
GALE

San Diego • Detroit • New York • San Francisco • Cleveland • New Haven, Conn. • Waterville, Maine • London • Munich

For more information, contact
The Gale Group, Inc.
27500 Drake Rd.
Farmington Hills, MI 48331-3535
Or you can visit our Internet site at http://www.gale.com

Photo credits: Cover © Blackbirch Press archives; pages 5, 7, 9 10, 11, 26, 28, 29 © North Wind Picture Archives; pages 8, 17, 18, 20, 24 © historypictures.com; pages 14, 21, 23 © Archiving Early America

LIBRARY OF CONGRESS CATALOGING-IN-PUBLICATION DATA
Parker, Lewis K.
  The Battle of Monmouth / by Lewis K. Parker.
      p. cm. — (Triangle history of the American Revolution series. Revolutionary War battles)
  Includes index.
  Summary: Describes the people and action of the Revolutionary War battle of Monmouth, New Jersey, which was the last battle fought between the two major armies, rather than by smaller forces.
  ISBN 1-56711-621-3 (hardback : alk. paper)
  1. Monmouth, Battle of, 1778—Juvenile literature. [1. Monmouth, Battle of, 1778. 2. United States—History—Revolution, 1775-1783—Campaigns.] I. Title. II. Series.
  E241.M7 P37 2003
  973.3'34—dc21   2002003373

Printed in China
10 9 8 7 6 5 4 3 2 1

CONTENTS

Preface: The American Revolution

Today, more than two centuries after the final shots were fired, the American Revolution remains an inspiring story not only to Americans, but also to people around the world. For many citizens, the well-known battles that occurred between 1775 and 1781—such as Lexington, Trenton, Yorktown, and others—represent the essence of the Revolution. In truth, however, the formation of the United States involved much more than the battles of the Revolutionary War. The creation of our nation occurred over several decades, beginning in 1763, at the end of the French and Indian War, and continuing until 1790, when the last of the original 13 colonies ratified the Constitution.

More than 200 years later, it may be difficult to fully appreciate the courage and determination of the people who fought for, and founded, our nation. The decision to declare independence was not made easily—and it was not unanimous. Breaking away from England—the ancestral land of most colonists—was a bold and difficult move. In addition to the emotional hardship of revolt, colonists faced the greatest military and economic power in the world at the time.

The first step on the path to the Revolution was essentially a dispute over money. By 1763, England's treasury had been drained in order to pay for the French and Indian War. British lawmakers, as well as England's new ruler, King George III, felt that the colonies should help to pay for the war's expense and for the cost of housing the British troops who remained in the colonies. Thus began a series of oppressive British tax acts and other laws that angered the colonists and eventually provoked full-scale violence.

The Stamp Act of 1765 was followed by the Townshend Acts in 1767. Gradually, colonists were forced to pay taxes on dozens of everyday goods from playing cards to paint to tea. At the same time, the colonists had no say in the passage of these acts. The more colonists complained that "taxation without representation is tyranny," the more British lawmakers claimed the right to make laws for the colonists "in all cases whatsoever." Soldiers and tax collectors were sent to the colonies to enforce the new laws. In addition, the colonists were forbidden to trade with any country but England.

Each act of Parliament pushed the colonies closer to unifying in opposition to English laws. Boycotts of British goods inspired protests and violence against tax collectors. Merchants who continued to trade with the Crown risked attacks by their colonial neighbors. The rising violence soon led to riots against British troops stationed in the colonies and the organized destruction of British goods. Tossing tea into Boston Harbor was just one destructive act. That event, the Boston Tea Party, led England to pass the so-called Intolerable Acts of 1774. The port of Boston was closed, more British troops were sent to the colonies, and many more legal rights for colonists were suspended.

Finally, there was no turning back. Early on an April morning in 1775, at Lexington Green in Massachusetts, the first shots of the American Revolution were fired. Even after the first battle, the idea of a war against England seemed unimaginable to all but a few radicals. Many colonists held out hope that a compromise could be reached. Except for the Battle of Bunker Hill and some minor battles at sea, the war ceased for much of 1775. During this time, delegates to the Continental Congress struggled to reach a consensus about the next step.

During those uncertain months, the Revolution was fought, not on a military battlefield, but on the battlefield of public opinion. Ardent rebels—especially Samuel Adams and Thomas Paine—worked tirelessly to keep the spirit of revolution alive. They stoked the fires of revolt by writing letters and pamphlets, speaking at public gatherings, organizing boycotts, and devising other forms of protest. It was their brave efforts that kept others focused on liberty and freedom until July 4, 1776. On that day, Thomas Jefferson's Declaration of Independence left no doubt about the intentions of the colonies. As John Adams wrote afterward, the "revolution began in hearts and minds not on battlefield."

As unifying as Jefferson's words were, the United States did not become a nation the moment the Declaration of Independence claimed the right of all people to "life, liberty, and the pursuit of happiness." Before, during, and after the war, Americans who spoke of their "country" still generally meant whatever colony was their home. Some colonies even had their own navies during the war, and a few sent their own representatives to Europe to seek aid for their colony alone while delegates from the Continental Congress were doing the same job for the whole United States. Real national unity did not begin to take hold until the inauguration of George Washington in 1789, and did not fully bloom until the dawn of the 19th century.

The Minuteman statue stands in Concord, Massachusetts.

The story of the American Revolution has been told for more than two centuries and may well be told for centuries to come. It is a tribute to the men and women who came together during this unique era that, to this day, people the world over find inspiration in the story of the Revolution. In the words of the Declaration of Independence, these great Americans risked "their lives, their fortunes, and their sacred honor" for freedom.

5

Introduction:
"So Superb a Man"

June 28, 1778, was a day much like earlier days that month in eastern New Jersey. Blistering heat and high humidity baked the countryside. Temperatures reached 100° F by noon. For the British soldiers who were marching across the state from Philadelphia to New York, it was difficult to put one foot in front of the next. Although they had rested at Monmouth Courthouse for two days before the final push to New York, the heat made marching in scratchy wool uniforms a hellish torture. To make matters worse, the Continental army, which had followed them, was now close enough to attack.

Ten days earlier, on June 18, General Henry Clinton, the British commander, had begun to move his army out of Philadelphia. He had been ordered to cross New Jersey to New York City, a Loyalist stronghold.

Clinton's army consisted of about 9,000 troops and 1,000 Loyalist supporters. A wagon train that carried food, ammunition, and other supplies extended 12 miles behind them.

As soon as the British left Philadelphia, General George Washington and his army had begun their pursuit of Clinton. While the British troops marched in the terrible heat, Washington slipped patrols ahead of them, and ordered the patrols to burn bridges and dump dirt into wells along the route.

In the muggy weather, sudden thunderstorms turned roads into mucky swamps. The pace of the British army slowed to a crawl. Wagons sank in the mud. The journey became a death march, as dozens of soldiers suffered heat stroke and fell beside the road.

Washington was cautious with his main force as he followed Clinton. Though the American and British armies were close in numbers, Washington did not want to risk an all-out battle. Instead, in late June, he sent half of his army to attack the British from the rear as soon as the British moved from Monmouth Courthouse. The movement began on June 28. Clinton, however, remained behind with a small force at the courthouse to keep the harassing Continentals off his back. Early in the morning, General Charles Lee's Americans met the soldiers at the courthouse.

Washington took command from Lee in the heat of the battle.

Clinton ordered his men to attack Lee's right flank. In the heat of battle, Lee became confused about the direction from which the attack was coming and ordered a retreat.

Washington, who had doubts about Lee's command abilities, arrived at the scene and saw panicked Americans dashing past him to the rear. They were retreating, but they had no idea why they were doing so.

Washington was enraged and ordered Lee to leave the field. The great general then halted his fleeing men and rallied them to battle as bullets whistled past his head. On this brutally hot day, Washington needed every bit of his personal power to keep discipline among his troops.

Writing afterward of General Washington on his horse amidst the clamor of battle, a young French officer, Marquis de Lafayette, wrote "His presence stopped the retreat. . . . I thought . . . I had never beheld so superb a man."

7

Retreat to Valley Forge

General William Howe commanded the British forces in America.

The last half of 1777 was among the worst periods of the American Revolution for the Continental army. On July 20, 1777, General William Howe, commander of the British forces in America, sailed out of New York Harbor on a secret mission to capture Philadelphia, the meeting place of the Continental Congress and the capital of the United States. On August 23, he landed his army near Elkton, Maryland. General George Washington recognized Howe's intent and marched his army south from Middle Brook, New Jersey, to guard Philadelphia from attack.

Washington set his men at Chad's Ford, Pennsylvania, on Brandywine Creek. On September 11, the British defeated the Americans at Brandywine. Nine days later, the Americans were defeated again at Paoli, Pennsylvania. From Paoli, Howe marched his army into Philadelphia on September 26. The Continental Congress had left the city and fled south to York, Pennsylvania, just before Howe's troops arrived. Once in Philadelphia, Howe placed 9,000 soldiers at Germantown, north of the city, 3,000 across the Delaware River in New Jersey, and about 9,000 in Philadelphia.

Washington's attempt at a surprise attack at Germantown on October 4 failed due to problems coordinating the arrival of various American units. The well-disciplined British troops, not surprised by the American attack, easily took control of the field.

After the battle, Howe withdrew his men to winter quarters in the safety of Philadelphia. Washington chose an area about 20 miles north of Philadelphia for his winter quarters. He led his soldiers westward from their location in Whitemarsh, marching through rain and sleet. On December 16, 1777, the tired and battered Continental army made camp at Valley

In late 1777, Washington led his troops to Valley Forge.

Who Were the American Soldiers?

★ ★ ★ ★ ★

American soldiers were short of supplies throughout the war.

Washington's army had three classes of soldiers. The Continentals were the regular members of the army. The standing militia were made up of soldiers from local groups, which usually included all able-bodied men from sixteen to sixty-five. The state troops were volunteers who served in the early years of the war. The militia thought of themselves mainly as an armed guard who defended their homes. They did not like to march or dig trenches.

After 1777, most Continental soldiers were from the poorer segments of society. Many joined the army because they had been promised free land when the war ended. Life in the army was usually not much better—and often worse—than their life on the farm or the city. During their time in the army, they faced diseases such as smallpox and yellow fever. Their food consisted mostly of beef and hard biscuits.

Although he was a stern commander who maintained a personal distance from his troops, Washington was deeply appreciative of them. "To see men without clothes to cover their nakedness," he wrote, "without blankets to lay on, without shoes, by which their marches might be traced by the blood from their feet, and almost as often without provisions as with; marching through frost and snow, and at Christmas taking up their winter quarters within a day's march of the enemy, without a house or hut to cover them till they could be built, and submitting to it without a murmur, is a mark of patience and obedience which in my opinion can scarce be paralleled."

Forge, Pennsylvania. Thus began one of most terrible times in American military history.

Washington chose Valley Forge as the winter headquarters because it was close enough to Philadelphia to allow him to keep track of British movements. Another reason for the choice of Valley Forge was that Congress—and the new capital—was now located at York, to the west. Valley Forge was between Philadelphia and York, and Washington could protect the Congress. The valley itself was a wooded area about two miles long that could be easily defended. It lay in an area of rolling hills protected by bluffs on all its sides.

At Valley Forge, the soldiers first built about 1,000 log huts, working day and night in frigid weather. The huts were 16 feet long, 14 feet wide, and a little more than 6 feet high. Straw and earth were heaped over the frames to make roofs. Every hut had a chimney and fireplace. Twelve men lived in each hut.

11

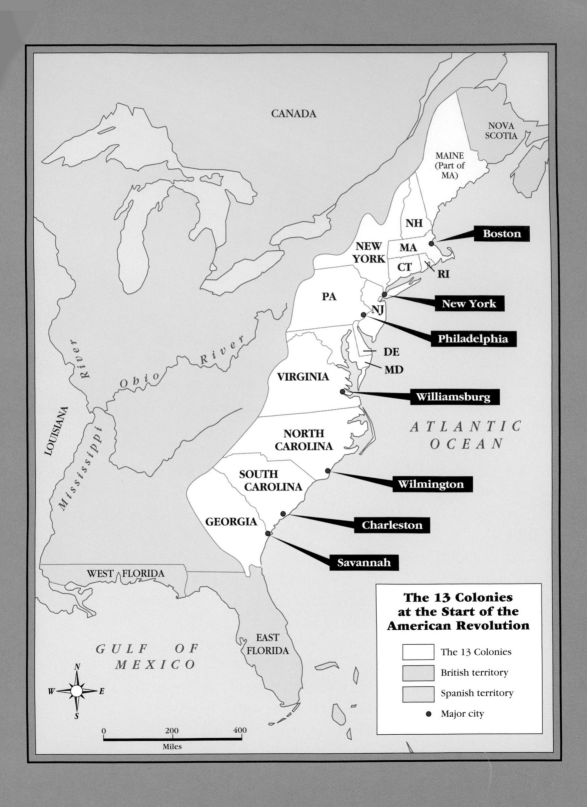

CANADA

NOVA
SCOTIA

MAINE
(Part of
MA)

NH

Boston

NEW
YORK

MA

CT

RI

PA

NJ

New York

Philadelphia

DE

MD

VIRGINIA

Williamsburg

*ATLANTIC
OCEAN*

NORTH
CAROLINA

SOUTH
CAROLINA

Wilmington

GEORGIA

Charleston

Savannah

WEST FLORIDA

EAST
FLORIDA

*GULF OF
MEXICO*

LOUISIANA

Mississippi River

Ohio River

N
W E
S

0   200   400
Miles

The 13 Colonies
at the Start of the
American Revolution

☐	The 13 Colonies
☐	British territory
☐	Spanish territory
●	Major city

Besides unbearable cold and constant wind, soldiers faced other hardships. Almost one-third of the soldiers had no shoes, and most had no blankets or warm clothing. The lack of food was another serious problem. A bakehouse was built, but there was no flour with which to bake bread. The men had no fresh vegetables or fresh meat. The only meat available was salt pork.

The extreme hunger and cold left most soldiers too weak to fight off illnesses such as pneumonia and typhoid fever. During the month of February alone, about 7,000 men were sick and 290 died. About 10,000 men in all were quartered at Valley Forge—and about 2,500 of them died of illness and disease over the winter.

Finally, as winter lifted in March 1778, some food began to arrive at Valley Forge. Although the men ate just one big meal a day, it might consist of nourishing steak, potatoes, and hickory nuts. As the nearby creeks and rivers thawed, the soldiers were also able to catch fish.

The only benefit of the bitter winter at Valley Forge was that it allowed time to train the unskilled Continental army. The primary drillmaster was Frederick Steuben, better known as the Baron von Steuben. The baron transformed Washington's army into a superb fighting force able to use 18th century battlefield techniques.

Von Steuben reached Valley Forge in February 1778. Although he had only been a captain in his native Prussia, he told Washington that he had held the rank of lieutenant general. He was not a real baron, either. None of that mattered, however, because von Steuben had been a soldier from the age of 16. He knew that the American troops needed training to fight effectively in the open in the style of European soldiers against the British.

Von Steuben, who came to America as a volunteer, served at first without rank in the army. He reported directly to

British troops in Philadelphia were well-supplied with food by farmers who charged high prices.

13

Baron von Steuben taught the Americans battle techniques used in Europe.

Washington, who eventually named him a major general and then inspector-general. Washington put von Steuben to work by asking him to pick some of the regiments and train them to fight the British.

The baron drilled the men in basic movements such as right turn, left turn, and about face. He taught them how to march in columns and how to hold the line of battle. Von Steuben showed soldiers how to fire their muskets and reload quickly, and trained them in shooting as a group for the most effective firepower. Finally, he trained the men in how to use bayonets in close combat.

Because von Steuben did not speak English, Captain Benjamin Walker translated the baron's commands— along with his insults about the men's lack of ability. Despite the language barrier, von Steuben proved to be a brilliant instructor. He drilled a small squad while a large company stood and watched. Then he switched and drilled the larger group while the smaller group observed. He also made officers drill their own men, and he expected officers to know the names of the men who served under them.

The men trained throughout the winter, and by spring they formed a tight, well-organized army. On March 24, von Steuben put on a demonstration that involved all the soldiers in Washington's army. He carried out maneuvers with 10 and 12 battalions. Though there were many divisions and regiments, they moved as one disciplined group. Finally, Washington had what he always wanted—a trained army.

Springtime Changes

By April, the weather had grown warmer, and the snow had disappeared. The mere sight of spring blossoms boosted the men's morale. Washington's spirits, however, were not high.

Weapons of the Revolution

Most American troops carried the smoothbore flintlock musket. This was not the most efficient of weapons; the musket ball was often not the same size as the bore, so the musket ball bounced along inside the barrel when the gun was fired. It is estimated that about one ball in 300 hit its target. For that reason, the muskets were most effective when used by soldiers in close formation where they could blast a wall of lead at the enemy. The guns were also most effective when the men fired off many shots in a short period of time. As a result, having soldiers assemble in firing lines, in which they fired then stepped back to reload as another line stepped forward, was the most common battlefield technique at that time. The musket barrel was also designed to be fitted with a bayonet—a sharp knifelike weapon—that could be used in charges and close combat.

Many Continental soldiers carried a long rifle called the Pennsylvania rifle or the Kentucky rifle. With its long barrel and rifle bore, this weapon could shoot farther than a musket and was much more accurate. A good marksman could hit his target at 100 yards, compared to half that distance for a musket. The rifle's drawback was that it took longer to load than a musket. A bayonet could not be attached to the long rifle either, thus the gun could only be swung as a club in close combat.

The British held Philadelphia, and the Continental army was unlikely to dislodge it. "Our present situation . . . is beyond description, irksome, and dangerous," he wrote in a letter.

The end of April finally brought good news to Washington—France had recognized the independence of the United States. The two countries had agreed to treaties that obligated France to help the colonies win their war. In return, the Americans were obliged to help France if a war occurred between France and Great Britain. Finally, neither country could agree to peace with Great Britain without the consent of the other.

After France had recognized the United States as an independent country, Washington wrote, "Calmness and serenity seems likely to succeed in some measure those dark and tempestuous clouds which at times appeared ready to overwhelm us. The game, whether well or ill played hitherto, seems now to be verging fast to a favorable issue." He set May 6, 1778, as a day of celebration.

★

Benjamin Franklin and John Adams were ministers to France in 1778.

★

Changes were also taking place in Philadelphia. On March 27, British soldiers learned that Sir Henry Clinton was replacing Howe as King George III's commander in chief for the American campaign. Clinton had been Howe's second in command.

Soon after taking over command, Clinton received word that a huge French fleet had sailed to help the Americans. He feared that the fleet would blockade the Delaware River and trap his army in Philadelphia, so he gave up control of the city. He sent most of his cavalry and artillery, two regiments of troops, and about 3,000 Tories—Americans loyal to the crown—to New York by sea. He decided to march the remainder of his army, about 9,000 troops, across New Jersey to New York City. The army's supply train of 1,500 wagons stretched for miles behind the marching troops.

The Battle of Monmouth

Sir Henry Clinton

Clinton was born in
Newfoundland, Canada.

From an early age, Sir Henry
Clinton was at the center of power.
He was the son of a high-ranking
British army officer. Because his
father served as the royal governor
of New York, Clinton lived in
America for the first eight years of
his life. At the age of 19, he
entered the British army and
fought in both King George's War
and the Seven Years' War. By the
1770s, he was a major general and
also sat in Parliament's House of
Commons. His life was marked by
tragedy. His wife died in child-
birth, which caused him to fall
into a deep depression. In 1775,
Clinton came to America with
Howe. He served as Howe's second
in command for 30 months.

Clinton enjoyed taking hikes and
traveling by canoe. He also liked to
study flowers and birds. His real
interest was playing musical
instruments, especially the violin.
His enjoyment of solitary activities,
rather than the normal drinking
and games of his fellow officers,
made him a hard man for those
under his command to get to
know.

Philadelphia was an important center of shipbuilding during the Revolution.

Almost as soon as the British left Philadelphia to cross New Jersey, American troops were on the move from Valley Forge. The soldiers marched north toward the Delaware River, and crossed it about 40 miles north of Philadelphia. Washington planned to pursue and harass Clinton across New Jersey. He sent squads ahead of the British to create obstacles that slowed the march. One group of 25 men did nothing but cut trees across the roads in front of the British army. This strategy gave the Americans time to catch up to the British and allowed for the possibility of a rear-guard attack.

Race Against Time

The large British force moved slowly—usually only five or six miles a day. A heat wave had struck in June, and daily, the temperature climbed to almost 100° F by noon. The heat was

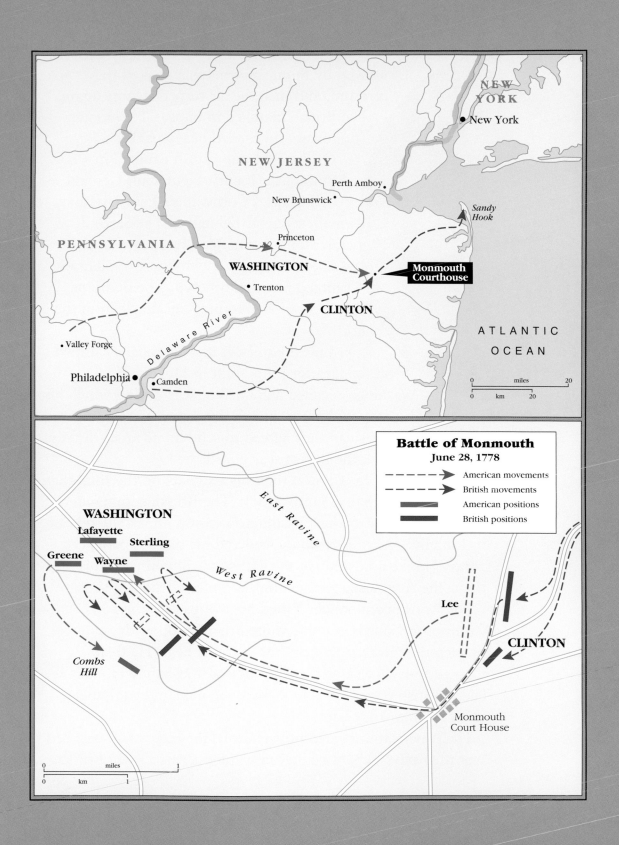

NEW
YORK

● New York

NEW JERSEY

Perth Amboy ●

New Brunswick ●

*Sandy
Hook*

PENNSYLVANIA

Princeton ●

WASHINGTON

● Trenton

CLINTON

Monmouth
Courthouse

Delaware River

● Valley Forge

ATLANTIC
OCEAN

Philadelphia ●

● Camden

| miles | 20 |
| km | 20 |

Battle of Monmouth
June 28, 1778

→ American movements
→ British movements
American positions
British positions

WASHINGTON

Lafayette

Sterling

Greene

Wayne

East Ravine

West Ravine

Lee

CLINTON

*Combs
Hill*

Monmouth
Court House

| miles | 1 |
| km | 1 |

followed by thunderstorms that soaked the ground, and then the air turned steamy again. The British marched in unbearable woolen uniforms and carried heavy packs.

On June 24, the British camped in Monmouth County. Lieutenant General Lord Charles Cornwallis's First Division made camp at Eglington. The Second Division, commanded by Lieutenant General Baron Wilhelm von Knyphausen, camped near Imlaystown. The divisions were positioned to prevent attack from the north.

On June 23 and 24, the Americans camped on the farm of John Hunt in Hopewell. Washington called a council of war during which his officers voted not to attack the enemy with a full force. Instead they agreed to send an advance division to attack the British rear guard.

Cornwallis was a close friend of King George III.

Early on June 25, Clinton took his redcoats on the road that led to Monmouth and Sandy Hook. The British commander had received reports that Washington would attack the rear of his long line. At Allentown, he ordered his most experienced troops to take a position at the end of the column. By this point, the Americans were within 20 miles of the British army.

The British commander halted his troops on June 26 at Monmouth Courthouse. He waited there another day to give his men time to recover from the extreme heat. He then planned to push east to the Atlantic coast at Sandy Hook. There British transport would carry the men and equipment north to New York City.

The Americans, located northwest of the redcoats, disagreed over their next step. Washington wanted to attack the British, but his council of generals voted against a direct attack three times. The flat, open land of that region of New Jersey favored the British fighting style. Instead, they suggested that Americans simply continue to harass the enemy. For his part, Washington knew that this would be his only chance he would have to corner Clinton and possibly destroy a huge portion of the British army. He pointed out that since the British were only 15 miles from the coast, there would be little time or opportunity to harass the redcoats enough to cause serious damage.

Washington was still considering his next move when he learned that the British were assembling to move out the next morning. That was all the information he needed—he decided to strike.

The American general's plan was to send about 5,500 troops—close to 80 percent of his force—to attack Clinton's rear guard. The remainder of the army would follow but would stay out of action unless needed. Washington chose General Charles Lee, the senior American general, to lead the advance group. It was a somewhat reluctant choice, because Lee had voted against attacking the British directly. At first, Lee refused to lead the soldiers. Washington then chose Lafayette.

Lafayette was wounded at the Battle of Brandywine in 1777.

Lafayette was not quite 21 years old and, although he was enthusiastic, his command experience was limited. The young Frenchman decided to march his men through the night and attack at dawn on June 27. He lost contact with Washington in the darkness, however, and had no idea where Washington and the main army were located. He also was uncertain exactly where the British troops were situated. As soon as Washington heard about Lafayette's predicament, he realized that the young man was not ready to lead troops. He ordered the force to rejoin the main force.

Embarrassed at almost being outdone by a young Frenchman, Lee now asked to be given command of the forces. On June 27, Lee took over for Lafayette at Englishtown. In addition to the regular army, about 900 New Jersey militia were stationed at Englishtown, about five miles northwest of Monmouth.

The Continentals numbered about 4,600 men under Lee. The number increased to 4,800 when 200 men under Colonel Henry Jackson of Boston arrived. With the New Jersey militia also under Lee's command, his total force was about 5,600 officers and men.

Washington and the main army stayed at Cranbury, about four miles behind Lee's soldiers. The commander was concerned about the distance. His large force was separated from Lee by deep ravines, which might prevent him from aiding Lee.

Behind British lines, the rear guard, commanded by Cornwallis, had taken up defensive positions northwest and southwest of the courthouse. Clinton had set up headquarters in the home of Elizabeth Covenhoven, an elderly widow whose house was on the western outskirts of the village. Clinton had chosen this area to rest and resupply because the surrounding farms were large, and food would be plentiful.

On the evening of June 27, Clinton made plans to march out the next morning toward Middletown and Sandy Hook. He gave orders that the Second Division would begin marching at three o'clock in the morning with the First Division following at five o'clock.

Meanwhile, on June 27, Washington moved his army from Cranbury to Ponolopon Bridge, about two and a half miles west of Lee's men at Englishtown. Once his men were in place, Washington rode into Englishtown to talk with Lee. Washington

The Battle of Monmouth

explained that he wanted the enemy to be attacked the next morning, June 28. Lee offered to assemble his staff officers for a five o'clock meeting.

At this meeting, Lee said that the exact number and location of the British army was not known. He added that he had not worked out plans for the battle, but that he would make plans when he came up against the enemy. Washington returned to his troops, concerned about Lee's lack of preparation but unwilling to cancel the attack.

"By God They Shall Do It!"

As the sun rose on June 28, General Philemon Dickinson, commander of the New Jersey militia, reported to Lee that he had engaged Clinton's forces and claimed that he had forced the British back from their lines. Lee decided to move forward cautiously, still uncertain of the enemy's exact position. To make matters worse, he received conflicting reports. Some reports, from Dickinson and others, stated that the British were moving out. Other reports stated that the British were ready to counter any American attack.

Charles Lee did not have an overall battle plan.

Lee's mission was jeopardized by incomplete information. He knew that the British were falling back, because their supply train was on the move, but he did not know that the redcoats' rear guard was preparing to prevent him from attacking the supply train.

Lee decided to divide his force, and sent troops to the left and right to outflank the British rear guard. Lee held some troops back in the center of the maneuver to place direct pressure on the British. His men marched out to the left and

German soldiers—called Hessians—were hired by the British and were widely feared by the Patriots.

right flanks prepared to launch an attack, but they never received any further orders. In the center, Lee ordered General Anthony Wayne to feint an attack. He had neglected, however, to explain his plan to his generals before they rode off. Thus Wayne's men began to fire, and the troops on the flank were uncertain about what to do once the shooting started.

Behind British lines, Clinton believed that the American attack was aimed at his supply wagons. He saw American movement from the center, and decided to launch an attack at what he thought was the main column of the American army— the right flank. Clinton gambled that the other American flanks would be drawn over to give support. He quickly sent in more men to bolster the rear guard, then launched an attack on the Americans.

The movement of the British troops destroyed Lee's plan to surround the rear guard. With the Americans' right flank under attack, Lee ordered Lafayette to take his men from the center to the right to give support.

The battle had barely begun when the Cornwallis's units opened up with cannon fire at Lee's center units. Lee ordered

The Battle of Monmouth

these exposed troops to find cover so that they would not be killed on the wide open battlefield. Some of the men took cover in the nearby village of Monmouth.

Meanwhile, soldiers on the left flank saw the movement at the center, and thought that Lee had ordered a retreat. At the same time, an American artillery regiment moved back to the rear because it had run out of ammunition. With all this movement, the men on the left flank became confused—they started to move back too because they had received no orders.

At first, Lee did not understand why the left flank was falling back, but when he realized they were in fact retreating, he ordered his right flank to retreat too. Lee thought that he was saving his troops by moving them away from where he believed the enemy was attacking. Confusion spread rapidly, as the flanking forces started to retreat but no one knew why. Lafayette sensed that something was dreadfully wrong and sent for Washington.

At that point, in midmorning, Washington was still at his headquarters awaiting a report from Lee on the progress of the battle. When he received a vague message from Lee that he was "doing well enough," Washington became concerned and decided to ride to the front lines.

As he left his headquarters, Washington was shocked to see the roads crowded with American soldiers running for their lives. Alarmed, he sent his aides to find out why the soldiers were retreating. The aides quickly reported back that they could determine no reason for the retreat except that Lee had ordered it. A furious Washington galloped down the road to find Lee.

As he rode up to his fellow Virginian, Washington angrily asked Lee to explain why his men were retreating. Lee believed that he had saved his army from disaster, and stammered as he tried to answer. Washington repeated his question.

Lee groped for an explanation and finally said that his orders had not been followed. Then he said that he did not think

Clinton assigned his toughest troops to the rear guard.

25

WASHINGTON REPROVING LEE AT
MONMOUTH.

Washington ordered
Lee from the field.

Americans could stand up against British soldiers. Washington
was absolutely enraged with Lee. He yelled, "Sir, they are able
and by God they shall do it!"

At that moment, Washington's aides reported that the British
were closing in on the retreating men. The road toward
Englishtown was cut by a ravine over which the Americans had
to cross on a narrow footbridge. If the redcoats caught the

The Battle of Monmouth

retreating Americans before the bridge, they would be slaughtered.

To salvage the mission and save the endangered force, Washington ordered Lee's remaining troops into a defensive position to block the enemy's advance. The long hours of training under von Steuben now began to pay off as the men formed double lines, one kneeling and one standing, to fire musket volleys into the advancing British. As one double line fired, the men moved to the rear to reload, and another double line stepped forward. The wall of musket balls halted the British charge.

Clouds of gunsmoke rolled across the open fields near Monmouth as the sun rose overhead. Washington's men stood their ground until the troops that had fled in panic during the confusion reached safety, where they could regroup and return to the battle lines.

Throughout the intense heat and noise of battle, Washington rode among his men on the field, ignoring the musket balls and cannon shot. In a later recounting of the battle, Lafayette praised Washington for preventing an almost certain defeat:

"His graceful bearing on horseback, his calm and deportment which still retained a trace of displeasure...were all calculated to inspire the highest degree of enthusiasm."

By early afternoon, Washington had gained control of the narrow road back to Englishtown. With their general directing their movement under heavy fire, the Americans moved with precision. The once-ragged troops, drilled by the gruff Prussian officer, now matched the British move for move in the European style of battle.

Washington placed troops on both sides of the road and positioned cannons to fire down its length. The gun crews, as well trained as their infantry counterparts, worked smoothly:

Washington's horse, Nelson, was renowned for its calm during battles.

27

Molly Pitcher

A woman named Mary Ludwig Hays played an important role in the Battle of Monmouth. She was the wife of William Hays, an artilleryman from Pennsylvania. Mrs. Hays followed her husband's unit and had spent the winter before the Battle at Valley Forge with him. During the Battle of Monmouth, Mrs. Hays was in the thick of the fighting. She carried pitchers of water from a nearby stream to cool both the men and the cannon barrels, and, at one point, she threw a wounded soldier over her shoulder and carried him to safety.

When her husband was wounded, she took over his position in the gun crew, ramming the powder bags and shot down the barrel. At one point, a British cannon-ball passed between her legs and tore off part of her skirt, but she stayed at her post. After the battle, George Washington named her an honorary sergeant upon learning of her heroic service. By then she had already earned the nickname Molly Pitcher.

Molly Pitcher took on the hottest job on the gun crew.

A powder bag was rammed down the barrel, followed by a cannonball or containers of lead shot called canister. Next, a line of gunpowder was poured in a hole directly above the powder bag. At the command, the gunner lit the powder to fire the gun. Then a water-soaked swab was used to quell any sparks still burning in the barrel.

Over and over, the gun crews fired cannonballs and canister shot, and the heat from the big guns added to the furnacelike heat of the day. Men sank to the ground near death from heat exhaustion. During this phase of the battle, the legendary Molly Pitcher took her collapsed husband's place on a gun crew.

Clinton attacked the Americans with his best men, but the Patriots held the line. At one point, the British commander sent troops marching toward enemy lines in a bayonet attack. The Americans fixed their own bayonets and turned back the attack in a bloody encounter of slashing steel. Even at those times when a segment of the American lines were forced to fall back, they moved in orderly fashion and did not panic.

The Americans and British fought for the entire day in the longest and hottest battle of the Revolution. By five o'clock the sounds of gunfire and cannons began to diminish. The

American cavalry defeated British horsemen in the heat of battle.

29

Americans had not advanced, but they had held their own against crack British troops. As darkness came, fresh American troops arrived at the front lines prepared to carry the battle to the British.

The fighting, however, was finished. By nightfall, the British appeared to be settling into camp on the battlefield until morning. But at ten o'clock, Clinton ordered his men to fall out and follow the last wagons of the supply train. As the moon rose around eleven o'clock, the British silently left the field of battle.

Epilogue

Afterward, the British picked up their pace. They quickly arrived at Sandy Hook and were ferried by barge to New York City.

Several months later, Lee was court-martialed and found guilty. He was removed from serving in the army for a year. In 1780, he was dismissed from service.

Both sides lost about 350 men at the Battle of Monmouth. Neither side won the Battle of Monmouth—the Americans claimed the victory, but the British were able to continue their march to New York City. Washington was unable to destroy Clinton's army. He did prove, however, that his disciplined Continentals could stand up against the best that the British had to offer.

The Battle of Monmouth was the last battle fought between the two major armies. Afterward, the fighting was done between smaller forces, and the battlefields shifted to the southern colonies.

Glossary

artillery large weapons used by fighting forces that fall into three categories—guns or cannons, howitzers, and mortars

bayonet a long, knifelike weapon that is attached to the end of a musket barrel

blockade to isolate an enemy by means of troops or ships

commander a military leader, usually holding the rank of general

division a military grouping of between 6,000 and 8,000 soldiers or two to three brigades

Loyalist colonial citizen who remained loyal to England

militia civilian soldiers who train with other citizens of a community, region, or state

regiment a military unit smaller than a brigade and a division

Tory A colonist who was loyal to the British government

For More Information

Books

Bobrick, Benson. *Angel in the Whirlwind: The Triumph of the American Revolution*. New York: Simon & Schuster, 1997.

Carter, Alden R. *The American Revolution: War for Independence*. Danbury, CT: Franklin Watts, 1993.

Dolan, Edward F. *The American Revolution: How We Fought the War of Independence*. Brookfield, CT: Millbrook Press, 1995.

Stevenson, Augusta. *Molly Pitcher: Young Patriot*. New York: Simon & Schuster, 1993.

Web Sites

Battle of Monmouth
http://home.infi.net/~jceres/history/wh363.html
Learn about the Battle of Monmouth and its importance.

Washington v. Lee at Monmouth
http://americanhistory.about.com/library/prm/blwashintonlee4.htm
Learn about the dispute between generals Washington and Lee.

Index

The Battle of Monmouth